T0170441

OLIVES

OLIVES

Poems

A. E. Stallings

TRIQUARTERLY BOOKS
NORTHWESTERN UNIVERSITY PRESS
EVANSTON, ILLINOIS

TriQuarterly Books
Northwestern University Press
www.nupress.northwestern.edu

Copyright © 2012 by A. E. Stallings. Published 2012
by TriQuarterly Books/Northwestern University Press.
All rights reserved.

Printed in the United States of America

10   9   8   7   6   5   4   3   2   1

Library of Congress Cataloging-in-Publication Data
Stallings, A. E. (Alicia Elsbeth), 1968–
   Olives : poems / A.E. Stallings.
     p. cm.
   ISBN 978-0-8101-5226-7 (pbk. : alk. paper)
   I. Title.
   PS3569.T3197O45 2012
   811'.54—dc23

                        2011032756

∞ The paper used in this publication meets the minimum
requirements of the American National Standard for
Information Sciences—Permanence of Paper for Printed
Library Materials, ANSI Z39.48-1992.

for my Argonauts

CONTENTS

OLIVES

I

The Argument

Olives

Sometimes a craving comes for salt, not sweet,
For fruits that you can eat
Only if pickled in a vat of tears—
A rich and dark and indehiscent meat
Clinging tightly to the pit—on spears

Of toothpicks maybe, drowned beneath a tide
Of vodka and vermouth,
Rocking at the bottom of a wide,
Shallow, long-stemmed glass, and gentrified,
Or rustic, on a plate cracked like a tooth,

A miscellany of the humble hues
Eponymously drab—
Brown greens and purple browns, the blacks and blues
That chart the slow chromatics of a bruise—
Washed down with swigs of barrel wine that stab

The palate with pine-sharpness. They recall
The harvest and its toil,
The nets spread under silver trees that foil
The blue glass of the heavens in the fall—
Daylight packed in treasuries of oil,

Paradigmatic summers that decline
Like singular archaic nouns, the troops
Of hours in retreat. These fruits are mine—
Small bitter drupes
Full of the golden past and cured in brine.

Jigsaw Puzzle

First, the four corners,
Then the flat edges.
Assemble the lost borders,
Walk the dizzy ledges,

Hoard one color—try
To make it all connected—
The water and the deep sky
And the sky reflected.

Absences align
And lock shapes into place,
And random forms combine
To make a tree, a face.

Slowly you restore
The fractured world and start
To re-create an afternoon before
It fell apart:

Here is summer, here is blue,
Here two lovers kissing,
And here the nothingness shows through
Where one piece is missing.

Recitative

Every night, we couldn't sleep—
Our upstairs neighbors had to keep
Dropping something down the hall—
A barbell or a bowling ball,

And from the window by the bed—
Scaling sharply in my head—
The alley cats expended breath
In arias of love and death.

Dawn again, across the street,
Jackhammers began to beat
Like hangovers, and you would frown—
That well-built house, why tear it down?

Noon, the radiator grill
Groaned, gave off a lesser chill
So that we could take off our coats.
The pipes coughed to clear their throats.

Our nerves were frayed like ravelled sleeves,
We cherished each our minor griefs
To keep them warm until the night
When it was time again to fight;

But we were young, did not need much
To make us laugh instead, and touch,
And could not hear ourselves above
The arias of death and love.

Sublunary

Midsentence, we remembered the eclipse,
Arguing home through our scant patch of park,
Still warm with barrel wine, when none too soon
We checked the hour by glancing at the moon,
Unphased at first by that old ruined marble
Looming like a monument over the hill,
So brimmed with light it seemed about to spill,

Then, there! We watched the thin edge disappear—
The obvious stole over us like awe
That it was our own silhouette we saw,
Slow perhaps to us moon-gazing here
(Reaching for each other's fingertips)
But sweeping like a wing across that stark
Alien surface at the speed of dark.

The crickets stirred from winter sleep to warble
Something out of time, confused and brief,
The roosting birds sang out in disbelief,
The neighborhood's stray dogs began to bark.
And then the moon was gone, and in its place,
A dim red planet hung just out of reach,
As real as a bitter orange or ripened peach

In the penumbra of a tree. At last
We rose and strolled at a reflective pace
Past the taverna crammed with light and smoke
And people drinking, laughing at a joke,
Unaware that anything had passed
Outside in the night where we delayed
Sheltering in the shadow we had made.

Four Fibs

1

Did
Eve
believe
or grapple
over the apple?
Eavesdropping Adam heard her say
to the snake-oil salesman she was not born yesterday.

2

Miss,
this
is not
Bliss. Wisdom
is not the abyss,
but visceral innocence. Kiss
the windfall of the world, she heard him whisper, or hiss.

3

Not
me,
not me!
cried all three.
"You shall creep the earth.
And you shall labor giving birth.
And as for you, you shall toil and sweat for all you're worth."

4

Cross
your
heart and
hope to die,
stick a needle in
your eye. That is the awful oath
of childhood, chapter and verse, genesis of the lie.

The Compost Heap

It waxed with autumn, when the leaves—
Dogwood, oak, and sycamore—
Avalanched the yard and slipped
Like unpaid bills beneath the door.

In winter it gave off a warmth
And held its ground against the snow,
The barrow of the buried year,
The swelling that spring stirred below.

In summer, we'd identify
The volunteers and green recruits,
A sapling apple or a pear
That stemmed from bruised or bitten fruits.

And everything we threw away
And we forgot, would by and by
Return to earth, or drop its seed
Take root and start to ramify.

We left the garden in the fall—
You turned the heap up with the rake
And startled latent in its heart
The dark glissando of a snake.

The Dress of One Occasion

The dress of one occasion in its box
Belongs to yesterday and to tomorrow—
But not to this day slowly turning yellow,
For better or worse, among the cotton flocks.

Disembodied now and ghostly pale,
Mummified in tissue easily torn
As though the flimsy pattern of a dress,
It's packed away—for what, you cannot guess—

Stored perhaps for someone not yet born
(You cannot see the face behind the veil)
The day of its occasion growing stale
And brittle as a triangle of cake—

Most innocent and decadent of frocks
Because solemn and frivolous—the fluff
That blows away from dandelion clocks,
The lace of time, that shifty, subtle stuff

That only time itself knows how to make
Out of the body's loom, the velvet marrow.
One Saturday in May, you thought the blue
Above your heads was yours to keep and new,

When really it was something old, to borrow.

Deus Ex Machina

Because we were good at entanglements, but not
Resolution, and made a mess of plot,
Because there was no other way to fulfill
The ancient prophecy, because the will
Of the gods demanded punishment, because
Neither recognized who the other was,
Because there was no difference between
A tragic ending and a comic scene,
Because the play was running out of time,
Because the mechanism of the sublime
To stay in working order needed using,
Because it was a script not of our choosing,
Because we were actors, because we knew for a fact
We were only actors, because we could not act

Telephonophobia

We joke about it. Really, you're annoyed
To make some call I should make on my own—

It doesn't bite, you say. That isn't true.
We keep it on a leash; it isn't tame.

It stalks us in our sleep. And when at last
Some shy, unbidden happiness arrives

That triggers its alarm, it's not for you.
I bring it to my head, it speaks my name:

Old anger pours like poison in my ear—
Or information, cool as dates on stone,

Rocks in its smooth, black cradle. I avoid
The thing, because it holds what I most fear:

At any hour, the future or the past
Can dial into the room and change our lives.

The Argument

After the argument, all things were strange.
They stood divided by their eloquence
Which had surprised them after so much silence.
Now there were real things to rearrange.
Words betokened deeds, but they were both
Lightened briefly, and they were inclined
To be kind as sometimes strangers can be kind.
It was as if, out of the undergrowth,
They stepped into a clearing and the sun,
Machetes still in hand. Something was done,
But how, they did not fully realize.
Something was beginning. Something would stem
And branch from this one moment. Something made
Them each look up into the other's eyes
Because they both were suddenly afraid
And there was no one now to comfort them.

Burned

You cannot unburn what is burned.
Although you scrape the ruined toast,
You can't go back. It's time you learned

The butter cannot be unchurned,
You can't unmail the morning post,
You cannot unburn what is burned—

The lovers in your youth you spurned,
The bridges charred you needed most.
You can't go back. It's time you learned

Smoke's reputation is well earned,
Not just an acrid, empty boast—
You cannot unburn what is burned.

You longed for home, but while you yearned,
The black ships smoldered on the coast;
You can't go back. It's time you learned

That even if you had returned,
You'd only be a kind of ghost.
You can't go back. It's time you learned

That what is burned is burned is burned.

On Visiting a Borrowed Country House
in Arcadia

for John

To leave the city
Always takes a quarrel. Without warning,
Rancors that have gathered half the morning
Like things to pack, or a migraine, or a cloud,
Are suddenly allowed
To strike. They strike the same place twice.
We start by straining to be nice,
Then say something shitty.

Isn't it funny
How it's what *has* to happen
To make the unseen ivory gates swing open,
The rite we must perform so we can leave?
Always we must grieve
Our botched happiness: we goad
Each other till we pull to the hard shoulder of the road,
Yielding to tears inadequate as money.

But if instead
Of turning back, we drive into the day,
We forget the things we didn't say.
The silence fills with row on row
Of vines or olive trees. The radio
Hums to itself. We make our way between
Saronic blue and hills of glaucous green
And thread

Beyond the legend of the map
Through footnote towns along the coast
That boast
Ruins of no account—a column
More woebegone than solemn—
Men watching soccer at the two cafés,
And half-built lots where dingy sheep still graze.
Climbing into the lap

Of the mountains now, we wind
Around blind, centrifugal turns.
The sun's great warship sinks and burns.
And where the roads without a sign are crossed,
We (inevitably) get lost.
Yet to be lost here
Still feels like being somewhere,
And we find

When we arrive and park,
No one minds that we are late—
There is no one to wait—
Only a bed to make, a suitcase to unpack.
The earth has turned her back
On one yellow middling star
To consider lights more various and far.
The shaggy mountains hulk into the dark

Or loom
Like slow, titanic waves. The cries
Of owls dilate the shadows. Weird harmonics rise
From the valley's distant glow, where coal
Extracted from the lignite mines must roll
On acres of conveyor belts that sing
The Pythagorean music of a string.
A huge grey plume

Of smoke or steam
Towers like the ghost of a monstrous flame
Or giant tree among the trees. And it is all the same—
The power plant, the forest, and the night,
The manmade light.
We are engulfed in an immense
Ancient indifference
That does not sleep or dream.

Call it Nature if you will,
Though everything that is is natural—
The lignite-bearing earth, the factory,
A darkness taller than the sky—
This out-of-doors that wins us our release
And temporary peace—
Not because it is pristine or pretty,
But because it has no pity or self-pity.

II

EXTINCTION OF SILENCE

Triolet on a Line Apocryphally Ascribed to Martin Luther

Why should the Devil get all the good tunes,
The booze and the neon and Saturday night,
The swaying in darkness, the lovers like spoons?
Why should the Devil get all the good tunes?
Does he hum them to while away sad afternoons,
And the long, lonesome Sundays? Or sing them for spite?
Why should the Devil get all the good tunes,
The booze and the neon and Saturday night?

Two Violins

One was fire-red,
Hand-carved and new—
The local maker pried the wood
From a torn-down church's pew,

The Devil's instrument
Wrenched from the house of God.
It answered merrily and clear
Though my fingering was flawed;

Bright and sharp as a young wine,
They said, but it would mellow,
And that I would grow into it.
The other one was yellow

And nicked down at the chin,
A varnish of Baltic amber,
A one-piece back of tiger maple
And a low, dark timbre.

A century old, they said,
Its sound will never change.
Rich and deep on G and D,
Thin on the upper range—

And how it came from the Old World
Was anybody's guess—
Light as an exile's suitcase,
A belly of emptiness:

That was the one I chose—
Not the one of flame—
And teachers turned in their practiced hands
To see whence the sad notes came.

Country Song

Death was something that hadn't happened yet.
I was driving in my daddy's pickup truck
At some late hour, the hour of broken luck.
It seeped up through the dashboard's oubliette,
Clear voice through murk—the radio was set
Halfway between two stations and got stuck.
But the words sobbed through, and I was suddenly struck
Like a gut string in the key of flat regret.

The voice came from beyond the muddy river—
You know the one, the one that's cold as ice.
Even then, it traveled like a shiver
Through my tributary veins—but twice
As melancholy to me now, because
I'm older than Hank Williams ever was.

Sabbatical

He has been underground
These seven years, but he will not rise
The way the cicadas will,
Punctual and shrill,
Casting off the gold film from their eyes,
Raptured out of their translucent shells
To stun
The leaded windows of their wings with sun,
Their voices riding on the heat like swells,
A rattling of broken bells,
Their sudden silence giant as a sound.

The Ghost Ship

She plies an inland sea. Dull
With rust, scarred by a jagged reef.
In Cyrillic, on her hull
Is lettered *Grief*.

The dim stars do not signify;
No sonar with its eerie ping
Sounds the depths—she travels by
Dead reckoning.

At her heart is a stopped clock.
In her wake, the hours drag.
There is no port where she can dock,
She flies no flag,

Has no allegiance to a state,
No registry, no harbor berth,
Nowhere to discharge her freight
Upon the earth.

Handbook of the Foley Artist

For the sound of distant thunder,
A father frowning,
For the smack of sarcasm,
Pop of bubblegum;

For a sudden summer downpour,
Sizzle of bacon,
For the sound of somewhere else,
Freight train at 2 A.M.;

For the sound of snoring,
Bees in the lilac bush.
For the sound of insomnia,
Eyelashes against a pillowcase;

For the sea's din,
Blood's hush in the cochlea of the ear,
For the screak of a seagull,
The playground's rusted swing;

For the sound of birth,
The radio between pangs,
For death,
Static of flies;

For dry bones,
Fig trees clattering in the wind,
For the vowel of the wind,
A dog left out in the yard;

Crumple paper
For the fricative of fire;
For the gasp of an opened letter,
Strike a match;

Take the telephone off the hook
For the sound of no answer.
For the sound of a broken heart,
Crack a joke.

Extinction of Silence

That it was shy when alive goes without saying.
We know it vanished at the sound of voices

Or footsteps. It took wing at the slightest noises,
Though it could be approached by someone praying.

We have no recordings of it, though of course
In the basement of the Museum, we have some stuffed

Moth-eaten specimens—the Lesser Ruffed
And Yellow Spotted—filed in narrow drawers.

But its song is lost. If it was related to
A species of Quiet, or of another feather,

No researcher can know. Not even whether
A breeding pair still nests deep in the bayou,

Where legend has it some once common bird
Decades ago was first not seen, not heard.

Blackbird Étude

for Craig Arnold

The blackbird sings at
the frontier of his music.
The branch where he sat

marks the brink of doubt,
is the outpost of his realm,
edge from which to rout

encroachers with trills
and melismatic runs sur-
passing earthbound skills.

It sounds like ardor,
it sounds like joy. We are glad
here at the border

where he signs the air
with his invisible staves,
TRESPASSERS BEWARE—

song as survival—
a kind of pure music which
we cannot rival.

Lines for Turner Cassity

Librarian with military bearing,
You've left us poems critics call unsparing,

A wit not merely clever but hard-bitten.
Sometimes I hear you utter *overwritten,*

And even at this distance, there's no choice
But hear the word in that distinctive voice,

Not circumflexing drawl, diphthonged legato,
But southern, brisk, particular staccato—

Inimitable voice—for never cruel—
Impatient only of the pompous *fool*

And vagueness that gesticulates at truth.
Clear and styptic as a dry vermouth,

You taught the courtesy of kindness meant
By shaming false and floral sentiment.

Death's crude arithmetic only exacts
The estimate of flesh and bone for tax;

You it has taken—and yet misconstrued—
For it has left us your exactitude.

Funereal Stelae: Kerameikos, Athens

In the Museum of Sorrow stand
The marble dead on either hand:
Each seated formally on a chair
In profile, with a mild, blank stare.
Others come to bid good-bye,
To shake hands, turn aside and cry
Into the folds of cloak or sleeve;
A huntsman leaves a hound to grieve,
Its tail tucked under, ears drooped low.
Sisters, brothers, parents go.
And everywhere, that silent noise,
The votaries of children's toys:
Clay dolls, tops with painted rings,
And four-wheeled horses pulled on strings.
Beyond the air-conditioned rooms,
The grassy suburbs of the tombs,
With tortoises humped here and there
Beside the foot-worn thoroughfare—
They hunker on these patchy lawns
Like scattered helmets made of bronze,
The verdigris of ancient war.
A stream meanders as before
Through reeds and stone, steady as grief
And graving Time, its low relief.

The Cenotaph
First Cemetery of Athens

The day I went to the First Cemetery
Looking for famous graves, the sky was blue
As wild irises in February
And there were mourners walking two by two
And gravediggers who had folk to bury
Along the cypress-vaulted avenue:
Priests and florists, all that's understood
In the solemn bustle of death's livelihood.

I came there seeking the adventurer,
The poet, the novelist, composer of song,
And though I had no map, yet I was sure
I'd come upon them if I wandered long
Among the plaques and formal portraiture,
The rows of marble headstones hundreds strong,
Eponymous mausoleums with their claim
To immortality, at least in name.

Then in the lesser alleys of the dead
Among the graven years mumbled with moss,
I felt somebody watching and turned my head,
And there a small girl stood, as at a loss,
And looked at me, as if something I'd read
Aloud was too loud, as if she might toss
Her curls and put her hands upon her hips,
But pressed instead a finger to her lips

To say, "Don't wake them," and she seemed to smile
To find herself and someone else alone
Sharing a secret for a little while,

Though I could walk away and she was stone.
I could not find among the rank and file
Among the rude democracy of bone
Any of the famous men I sought
Although I scanned the legends plot by plot.

But I found widows bent over the task
Of tending shrines, and women washing the grime
Patiently from angels who wore a mask
Where acid rain turned marble into lime.
A woman stopped me on the path to ask—
As someone asks a stranger for the time—
Where she could find the Sleeper, to lay a rose
Upon that breathless beauty's long repose.

But roaming lost amidst death's anterooms,
I did not find the exile or his bust,
Nor the swashbuckling ransacker of tombs
Who sifted stories for the golden dust
Of kings and queenly ladies at their looms,
All that was not devoured by moth or rust;
Nor the composer, nor the novelist.
The more I looked for them, the more I missed—

It was the grave of nobody I sought—
It was the purling of the ash-gray dove
In cypress boughs, and plastic flowers bought
To be the token of undying love
Some twenty years ago—they could not rot
But faded to a kind of garish mauve
Just like the fading afternoon—while I
Wandered between two dates, and earth and sky.

Pop Music

for a new parent

The music that your son will listen to
To drive you mad
Has yet to be invented. Be assured,
However, it is approaching from afar
Like the light of some Chaldean star.

On what new instruments of torture, through
What waves, lasers, wires, telepathy,
The same banalities will play
Systolic and diastolic as before,
It's hard to say—

As for the lyrics, or the lack thereof,
About love or about the lack of love,
Despite the heart's reputed amputation,
They will be as repetitive as sex
Without the imagination.

The singers will appall you, yes,
With their outlandish dress or lack of dress
Or excess hair or lack of hair, tattoos,
All aspects of their hygiene, because they remind you that he spends
Too many hours with hooligans called friends,

And while you knit another ugly sweater,
The pulsars of the brave new tunes will boom
From the hormonal miasma of his room,
Or maybe they'll just beam into his brain—
Unheard melodies are better.

Thus it has always been. Maybe that's why
The sappy retro soundtrack of your youth
Ambushes you sometimes in a café
At this almost-safe distance, and you weep, or nearly weep
For all you knew of beauty, or of truth.

III

THREE POEMS FOR PSYCHE

Advice to Psyche
hem audax et temeraria lucerna

Resist the ugly sisters and their wisdom.
They cannot hold a candle to your flame.
Keep your word so there will be no story;
A happy ending ends it just the same.

Be blind, uncurious. Resist the urge
To look upon Desire in the light—
Not lest it turn out monstrous, and dark—
But singed, and beautiful, and winged for flight.

The Eldest Sister to Psyche

This palace, those invisible hands
That stroke the music from thin air,
Call it magic: everywhere
The haunted rooms obey commands,
And yet it sounds like loneliness.
Yes, I'm that ugly sister, true,
You'll say I only envy you.
The fact—I know your secret guess—
Surrendered blind to his embrace,
You dared not look. A human voice,
You thought. You never had a choice.
Perhaps a monster, face-to-face,
With scales and fangs and leathern wings.
What of the fetus that you carry?
For certain it is human? Very?
Doubt burns like hot wax; it stings.

Doubt burns. Like hot wax, it stings.
For certain, it is human, very.
What of the fetus that you carry,
With scales and fangs and leathern wings
Perhaps? A monster. Face-to-face,
You thought you never had a choice,
You dared not. Look, a human voice
Surrendered blind to his. Embrace
The fact. I know your secret. Guess.
You'll say I only envy you.
Yes I'm that ugly, Sister True,
And yet . . . It sounds like loneliness,
The haunted rooms. Obey commands:
Call it magic. Everywhere,
That stroke, the music. From thin air,
This palace, those invisible hands.

The Boatman to Psyche, on the River Styx

But I have one last errand for you, my poppet.
    —*Apuleius,* The Golden Ass

Only a few have come here still alive:
Heroes seeking immortality,
Lovers who refuse to grieve.

They are found out by gravity,
How they unbalance the scow
With one foot still on the quay

And the other stepping into the prow
While evil-smelling bilge comes seeping
Up through the planks, as it is doing now.

The sorry hound is usually sleeping
(Three heads, no brain),
But his job is keeping

The inmates in. He has no reason
To keep the living out.
All will come here in their own sweet season.

Perhaps you thought
No one would notice you among so many,
But you are not the shadow of a doubt,

You are the thing itself. Your shiny penny
Will pay your passage, though it should be double.
You are two if you are any—

You quibble?
Aren't you a double tug upon
The earth, and twice the trouble?

Gravid girl, you're far gone.
I feel the quickening,
Obscene here where all frenzy is done,

Sickening,
A thing like that, a specter that looms
Out of the queasy future, ticking and ticking

Like a kind of bomb.
An X-ray developing in your chemical bath,
Your dark room.

You wonder how a blind man finds his path
Over the swamp of hate,
The river of wrath?

My eyes are ultrasound. I echolocate
Like the pipistrelles that drop
Their slick of guano on the sloping slate—

Treacherous footing. Here's our stop.
So, you're on an errand to the Queen,
To borrow her beauty like a pot of makeup.

It's true that she has stayed just seventeen:
The sun can't spoil her looks—
Her lips are stained with grenadine,

And here there are only stopped clocks
And no reflections. A hint:
If she gives you a wooden box

Yea big—scarcely big enough for an infant—
Don't open it, though you crave
A peek, a free sample. You say you won't,

But the living have a flair for narrative.
What if I tell you all the beauty ever worn
By loveliness was borrowed from the grave

And belongs to the unborn?

Persephone to Psyche

Come sit with me here at the bar.
Another Lethe for the bride.
You're pregnant? Well, of course you are!
Make that a Virgin Suicide.

Me and my man, we tried a spell,
A pharmacopoeia of charms,
And yet . . . When I am lonesome, well,
I rock the stillborns in my arms.

This place is dead—a real dive.
We're past all twists, rewards and perils.
But what the hell. We all arrive.
Here, have some pomegranate arils.

I heard an old wives' tale above
When I was a girl with a girl's treasure.
The story went, Soul married Love
And they conceived, and called her Pleasure.

In Anhedonia we take
Our bitters with hypnotic waters.
The dawn's always about to break
But never does. We dream of daughters.

IV

FAIRY-TALE LOGIC

Fairy-Tale Logic

Fairy tales are full of impossible tasks:
Gather the chin hairs from a man-eating goat,
Or cross a sulfuric lake in a leaky boat,
Select the prince from a row of identical masks,
Tiptoe up to a dragon where it basks
And snatch its bone; count dust specks, mote by mote,
Or learn a phone directory by rote.
Always it's impossible what someone asks—

You have to fight magic with magic. You have to believe
That you have something impossible up your sleeve—
The language of snakes, perhaps; an invisible cloak,
An army of ants at your beck, or a lethal joke,
The will to do whatever must be done:
Marry a monster. Hand over your firstborn son.

The Catch

Something has come between us—
It will not sleep.
Every night it rises like a fish
Out of the deep.

It cries out with a human voice,
It aches to be fed.
Every night we heave it weeping
Into our bed,

With its heavy head lolled back,
Its limbs hanging down,
Like a mer-creature fetched up
From the weeds of the drowned.

Damp in the tidal dark, it whimpers,
Tossing the cover,
Separating husband from wife,
Lover from lover.

It settles in the interstice,
It spreads out its arms,
While its cool underwater face
Sharpens and warms:

This is the third thing that makes
Father and mother,
The fierce love of our fashioning
That will have no brother.

Two Nursery Rhymes: Lullaby and Rebuttal

I. Lullaby for a Colicky Baby

For crying out loud,
It's only spilt milk.
The way your sharp cries rend
The air's thin silk,
The way your blue skies cloud
And take away our sun,
You'd think the world about to end
Instead of just begun.

II. Baby Talk

I have drunk all that I can of you,
The warm, white oblivion of sleep.
Now I spit you out. Now I eat—
Everything, even the dirt, goes in my mouth.
Whatever you forbid me I shall try;
The world is sour, bitter, salt, and sweet.
Now there is a sorrow you call teeth
That gnaws at me, that's cutting its way through.
You cannot comfort me. I used to weep,
But now I keen: I *sharpen* and I *cry*.

Containment

So long I have been carrying myself
Carefully, carefully, like a small child
With too much water in a real glass
Clasped in two hands, across a space as vast
As living rooms, while gazes watch the waves
That start to rile the little inland sea
(Slapping against its cliffs' transparency),
Revise and meet, double their amplitude,
Harmonizing doubt from many ifs.
Distant frowns like clouds begin to brood.
Soon there is overbrimming. Soon the child
Looks up to find a face to match the scolding,
And just as he does, the vessel he was holding
Is almost set down safely on the bookshelf.

Accident Waiting to Happen

for Finn

Like the scalding cup
Of coffee you left
At the brink of the table,

I brim with potential.
I'm bright and unstable
As a just-mopped floor,

I'm a curtain near a candle,
Finger in the door,
A loose axe handle.

I'm the wrist flicked fast
With no backwards look
Blindly casting

The innocent fishhook.
I'm the toy on the stair,
The hole in the street.

I'm right in plain sight,
I'm under your feet.
I'm over your head:

I've got an edge,
And I hang by a thread.
It's almost time,

And my aim is steady.
You're falling for me,
I feel it. I'm

Ready.

Dinosaur Fever

for Nicole, who was in a dinosaur book, and Jason,
who would like to be

Dinosaur fever—they all get it,
Kindergartners of either sex.
It'll drive you crazy if you let it—
Facts on *Tyrannosaurus rex,*

Triceratops, Iguanodon,
Stegosaurus, always a classic;
You must become an expert on
All things Cretaceous and Jurassic.

Tots tell you what things mean in Greek,
In tones superior and mammalian;
It seems they only just learned to speak
And now they speak sesquipedalian.

I'm not talking Barney, all goofy and purple,
Chubby and bouncy and eager for school,
But great scaly reptiles that bellow and hirple,
A jawful of daggers and bloody drool.

They're better than dragons and Fabulous Creatures:
Maybe a factor of their appeal
Is even the kindergarten teachers
Won't deny the brutes were *real.*

Kids like their titanomachies gory,
Giants hurtling toward disaster,
Extinction as Grimm bedtime story,
Life getting smaller, smarter, faster . . .

It's only a phase, this fad for fossil:
Soon kids evolve to another stage
(Barbie or Spiderman, hardly colossal).
Does something dawn on them at this age,

Some sudden awareness of time unsung,
Aeons when monsters stalked the earth;
How once even their parents were young
In that vast prehistory to their birth?

Tulips

These tulips make me want to paint:
Something about the way they drop
Their petals on the tabletop
And do not wilt so much as faint,

Something about their burnt-out hearts,
Something about their pallid stems
Wearing decay like diadems,
Parading finishes like starts,

Something about the way they twist
As if to catch the last applause,
And drink the moment through long straws,
And how, tomorrow, they'll be missed.

The way they're somehow getting clearer,
The tulips make me want to *see*—
The tulips make the other me
(The backwards one who's in the mirror,

The one who can't tell left from right),
Glance now over the wrong shoulder
To watch them get a little older
And give themselves up to the light.

Alice in the Looking Glass

No longer can I just climb through—the time
Is past for going back. But you are there
Still conning books in Hebrew, right to left,
Or moving little jars on the dresser top
Like red and white pieces on a chessboard. Still
You look up curiously at me when I pass
As if you'd ask me something—maybe why
I've kept you locked inside. I'd say because
That is where I'd have reflections stay,
In surfaces, where they cannot disquiet,
Shallow, for all that they seem deep at bottom;
Though it's to you I look to set things right
(The blouse askew, hair silvering *here* and *here*)
Where everything reverses save for time.

Umbrage

Persistent little sister
Always tagging along,
Aping your every gesture
Though getting the angle wrong,

Effacing, very thin,
Born when you were born,
A kind of grim twin
Never to be torn

Away, cooler and darker,
Always underfoot,
Impermanent magic marker
That won't stay put—

On bright days she appears
A fair-weather friend,
But she's dragged you through the years,
Faithful to the end:

She's nobody's lover or wife,
She was never the pretty one;
She clings to you, though all your life
You've been standing in her sun.

Hide and Seek

My son was pretending. He said, "I am a shadow!"
He did this simply by shutting his eyes:
Inhabiting the same space as his body
While keeping all the light from coming in.
I laughed and kissed him, though it chilled me a little,
How still he stood, giving darkness his shape.

Sea Girls

for Jason

"Not gulls, *girls*." You frown, and you insist—
Between two languages, you work at words.
(*R*'s and *l*'s, it's hard to get them right.)
We watch the heavens' flotsam: garbage-white
Above the island dump (just out of sight),
Dirty, common, greedy—only birds.
OK, I acquiesce, too tired to banter.

Somehow they're not the same, though. See, they rise
As though we glimpsed them through a torn disguise—
Spellbound maidens, wild in flight, forsaken—
Some metamorphosis that Ovid missed,
With their pale breasts, their almost human cries.
So maybe it is I who am mistaken;
But you have changed them. You are the enchanter.

Listening to *Peter and the Wolf* with Jason, Aged Three

Eyes wide open, grinning ear to ear,
Balanced between the thrill of fear and fear,
He clutches at my skirt to keep me near

And will not let me leave him by himself
In the living room where *Peter and the Wolf*
Emerges from the speakers on the shelf.

He likes Peter's jaunty swing of strings,
The reedy waddle of the duck, the wings
That flute up in the tree, but still he clings,

(Even though for now it's just the cat
Picking its sneaky way through sharp and flat);
He isn't frightened of a clarinet,

And laughs at Grandfather's bluster and bassoon,
But keeps his ear out for another tune
At the shadowy edge of the wood, and coming soon.

Where is the wolf? he asks me every chance
He gets, and I explain each circumstance;
Though it's not as if he's heard it only once—

You'd think he'd know by now. *Deep in the wood,*
Or under the tree, or sent away for good
To the zoo, I say, and think he's understood,

And weary of the question and the classic,
I ask *him* where the wolf is. With grave logic
He answers me, "The wolf is in the music."

And so it is. Just then, out of the gloom
The cymbal menaces, the French horns loom.
And the music is loose. The music's in the room.

The Mother's Loathing of Balloons

I hate you,
How the children plead
At first sight—

I want, I need,
I hate how nearly
Always I

At first say *no,*
And then comply.
(Soon, soon

They will grow bored
Clutching *your*
Umbilical cord)—

Over the moon,
Lighter-than-air,
Should you come home,

They'd cease to care—
Who tugs you through
The front door

On a leash, won't want you
Anymore
And will forget you

On the ceiling—
Admittedly,
A giddy feeling—

Later to find you
Puckered, small,
Crouching low

Against the wall.
O thin-of-skin
And fit to burst,

You break for her
Who wants you worst.
Your forebear was

The sack of the winds,
The boon that gives
And then rescinds,

Containing nothing
But the force
That blows everyone

Off course.
Once possessed,
Your one chore done,

You float like happiness
To the sun,
Untethered afternoon,

Unkind,
Marooning all
You've left behind:

Their tinfoil tears,
Their plastic cries,
Their wheedling

And moot good-byes,
You shrug them off—
You do not heed—

O loose bloom
      With no root
            No seed.

Another Bedtime Story

One day you realize it. It doesn't need to be said—
Just as you turn the page—*the end*—and close the cover—
All, all of the stories are about going to bed:

Goldilocks snug upstairs, the toothy wolf instead
Of grandmother tucked in the quilts, crooning *closer, closer*—
One day you realize it. It hardly needs to be said:

The snow-pale princess sleeps—the pillow under her head
Of rose petals or crystal—and dreams of a lost lover—
All, all of the stories are about going to bed;

Even the one about witches and ovens and gingerbread
In the dark heart of Europe—can children save each other?—
You start to doubt it a little. It doesn't need to be said,

But I'll say it, because it's embedded in everything I've read,
The tales that start with *once* and end with *ever after,*
All, all of the stories are about going to bed,

About coming to terms with the night, alleviating the dread
Of laying the body down, of lying under a cover.
That's why our children resist it so. That's why it mustn't be said:
All, all of the stories are about going to bed.

ACKNOWLEDGMENTS

My thanks to the editors of the following periodicals, in which these poems first appeared, sometimes in slightly different versions:

Able Muse: "Lines for Turner Cassity"

American Arts Quarterly: "Umbrage"

The Atlantic Monthly: "Olives" (the anagrammatic poem)

Beloit Poetry Journal: "Another Bedtime Story"

The Cortland Review: "The Argument," "Four Fibs" (A fib is a form invented by Gregory K. Pincus that uses the Fibonacci sequence to govern the number of syllables per line.)

The Formalist: "Country Song," originally titled "Long Gone Lonesome Blues" (Howard Nemerov Sonnet Award)

The Hudson Review: "Handbook of the Foley Artist," "Hide and Seek"

Linebreak: "Alice in the Looking Glass"

The National Poetry Review: "The Compost Heap"

The New Criterion: "Accident Waiting to Happen," "Deus Ex Machina," "Olives," "Pop Music"

New York Sun: "Baby Talk," "Telephonophobia"

Poetry: "Blackbird Étude," "The Catch," "Containment," "Extinction of Silence," "Fairy-Tale Logic," "The Mother's Loathing of Balloons," "On Visiting a Borrowed Country House in Arcadia," "Recitative," "Sublunary," "Triolet on a Line Apocryphally Ascribed to Martin Luther," "Tulips," "Two Violins"

Poetry.org: "Sea Girls"

Smartish Pace: "The Ghost Ship"

The Southern Review: "The Cenotaph"

Subtropics: "The Dress of One Occasion," "Listening to *Peter and the Wolf* with Jason, Aged Three"

Think Journal: "Funereal Stelae: Kerameikos, Athens"

32 Poems: "Burned," "Dinosaur Fever"

Unsplendid: "Sabbatical"

Valparaiso Poetry Review: "Three Poems for Psyche"

Thanks to Poetry Daily (www.poems.com) and Verse Daily (www.versedaily .com) for featuring several of these poems. Thanks to the House of Literature at Lefkes, Paros, for a two-week residency during which some of these poems were initiated. Also thanks to Dick Davis, Rachel Hadas, Mike Levine, Catherine Tufariello, and David Yezzi for their patience in looking over this manuscript. And as always *chilia eucharisto* to John Psaropoulos, my captive audience.